J. E Pollock

Lorenzo

And Other Poems

J. E Pollock

Lorenzo
And Other Poems

ISBN/EAN: 9783744714143

Printed in Europe, USA, Canada, Australia, Japan

Cover: Foto ©Thomas Meinert / pixelio.de

More available books at **www.hansebooks.com**

LORENZO

AND OTHER POEMS.

BY

J. E. POLLOCK, B.A.

TORONTO:
WILLIAM BRIGGS,
78 & 80 King Street East.

1883.

Entered according to the Act of the Parliament of Canada, in the year one thousand eight hundred and eighty-three, by J. E. POLLOCK, B.A., in the Office of the Minister of Agriculture, at Ottawa.

TO

M. M.

This Volume

IS INSCRIBED

BY

THE AUTHOR.

PREFACE.

IT is with some hesitation that these Poems are sent to the Press. In this age of "The Newspaper" and "The Novel," the Muses are neither much courted nor caressed, especially the serious or sentimental Muse.

Most of the Poems in this little volume—now published in book form for the first time—have already appeared in different periodicals; and, having met with some favor, I have been induced to collect, revise, and publish them in this form, believing that they will justly receive credit for any merit that may be found in them, and, at the same time, not doubting that they will receive whatever criticism they deserve.

J. E. P.

KESWICK, Feb. 23, 1883.

CONTENTS.

	PAGE
LEONORE	9
WHEN THE BRIGHT STARS ARE SHINING	12
JUNE	14
DECEMBER	16
LINES ON THE DEATH OF AN INFANT	18
CLEMENCY	20
HUMILITY	22
FELICITY	23
LOVE	29
FORTUNE	31
HOPE	34
THE FLOWERS	37
THE ROSE	39

CONTENTS.

	PAGE
THE WATER-LILY	41
THE STARS MAY SHINE	43
WOMAN'S INFLUENCE	45
IN MEMORIAM	50
LOST FEELINGS	55
THE CLOUDS	59
HOME	62
MAN'S INCONSTANCY	63
MEMORIES	65
SPRING	68
INDIAN SUMMER	70
MORN	72
GARFIELD—A SONNET	73
INDIA	74
BATTLE OF THE PLAINS OF ABRAHAM	77
WATERLOO	83
ALEXANDRIA	88
CHARGE OF THE HIGHLAND BRIGADE AT TEL-EL-KEBIR	92
LORENZO. PART I.—THE SHIPWRECK	95

LORENZO

AND OTHER POEMS.

LEONORE.

WHOSE voice is that so sweet I hear,
   Whose music is both sweet and clear
To please the heart and charm the ear?
  The voice of her whom I adore,
            Leonore.

Whose eyes are those serenely blue,
That speak a love so deep and true
No language can their depths construe?
  The eyes of her whom I adore,
            Leonore.

And whose those flowing locks of hair,
That fall around a neck so fair
No Parian marble may compare?
   The locks of her whom I adore,
        Leonore.

And whose that fair symmetric mould
Of classic features that unfold
The rival of the arts of old?
   The form of her whom I adore,
        Leonore.

Aurora rises fair to view
And gilds the glistening drops of dew,
But night and morn thine eyes renew
   Sweet charms to me forever more,
        Leonore.

The moon may gild the silent sea,
And spread her soft beams o'er the lea,
And waft her nightly charms to me;
   But thine's a charm forever more,
        Leonore.

The harp may breathe her sweet notes low,
But sweeter music yet I know—
The music from thy lips that flow,
   Surpassing sweetest strains of yore,
              Leonore.

E'en like the light winds fresh and free
That constant kiss the blooming lea
My thoughts go wandering unto thee—
   To thee both now and evermore,
               Leonore.

In thee life's sweetest charm I find;
In thee is every grace combined;
Thou fairest one of womankind,
   My own sweet love forever more,
               Leonore.

WHEN THE BRIGHT STARS ARE SHINING.

TO ⸺.

WHEN the bright stars are shining in heaven's deep blue,
And the moon o'er the waters her glimmerings renew,
Oft I think then, dear maiden, I think then of you;

And my mem'ries go drifting like waves of the sea
Back again to those bowers romantic and free,
Where so oft in my childhood I lingered with thee;

And the flowers we gathered, the wreaths we entwin'd
E'en have left their sweet fragrance still fresh in my mind,
But I sigh for the image my heart then enshrin'd.

Those bright days like their visions long since have decay'd;
And the future unfolding its sunshine and shade
Has reveal'd me the phantoms my childhood array'd.

But round my lone pillow 'mid the darkness of night
E'er thy vision shall linger—a halo of light—
To dispel 'mid my slumbers each phantom of fright.

JUNE.

AT the dawning of the morning
    In the pale light of the moon,
Day is looming like thy coming,
    Sweetest month of fairest June.

Like a vision, fair Elysian,
    Comest thou of all the year,
With sun-gilded skies up-builded—
    Golden seas in atmosphere;

With green mountains, crystal fountains,
    Azure lakes, and sunny isles,
With each river, rolling ever
    'Mid the Summer's sweetest smiles.

Gardens blooming meet thee coming
    With the flowers of thy choice;
All the ringing woodlands bringing
    Unto thee their sweetest voice.

JUNE.

As a virgin, just emerging,
  Woman's rights to soon command,
Dons the bridal at Love's Idol,
  And is entering Hymen's band,

So appearing, so endearing,
  Comest thou with smiles serene—
Youth and beauty, love and duty,
  Beaming in each brilliant scene.

Come, thou, smiling! come, beguiling
  Sorrows that are never thine!
Come with gladness, banish sadness,
  Fill our hearts with love divine!

DECEMBER.

NOW the dark and drear December—
    Icy monarch of the plain—
Grasps the sceptre of November,
    And begins his chilly reign;

And erects his sovereign power
    All across the temperate zone,
Where fair Summer built her bower
    And the glories of her throne;

Stills the rippling rill and river;
    Binds the frost-beleaguered lea;
Flings from out his icy quiver
    Darts across the inland sea:

And upon the hills and mountains—
    Once the scenes of Summer's bloom—
And beside the crystal fountains,
    There he spreads his wintry gloom.

DECEMBER.

Spreads beneath, around, and over
   Nature's groves and woodlands green,
Emblem sheets that lightly cover
   Forms enwrapp'd their folds between.

But beneath thy folds, December,
   Lie the embryonic gems
That from out their chilly chamber
   June shall woo with diadems.

LINES

ON THE DEATH OF AN INFANT.

HAPPY infant, gone to rest,
    Thou art number'd with the blest,
Care, nor woe, nor sin oppress'd,
Dwelt not in thy gentle breast.

Soon thy pure bright spirit fled;
Thou art number'd with the dead;
'Neath Death's mantle softly spread
Rests thy form in earth's cold bed.

Few the days that number'd here
Thy bright presence in this sphere,
Till upon thine infant bier
Sorrow dropp'd the silent tear.

But, sweet nursling, pure and fair,
Thou hast left a world of care
For celestial realms, where
Thou shalt heaven's blessings share.

LINES.

Free from each unholy stain,
Thou hast left a world of pain;
Well, thou didst not here remain,
Heaven is thine endless gain.

Sad we feel that thou art gone,
But we know thy spirit's flown
To that bright celestial zone,
Number'd with the blest alone;

Where amid the ransomed—free—
In their home Eternity,
We again, through grace, may see
Thee a child of purity.

CLEMENCY.

"O clementiam admirabilem, atque omni laude, predicatione, litteris monumentisque decorandum!"
—Cicero.

DEAREST boon to mortals given!
   Celestial daughter of the skies!
Coming from the highest heaven,
   Immortal hope within thee lies.

Mortals are but imperfection;
   To err is human not divine;
Tho' we know the right direction,
   To the wrong our souls incline.

Heaven's wisdom knows our weakness;
   God knows how much within us lives;
Love subdues the heart to meekness,
   But Mercy pities and forgives.

Lover of our soul's submission,
   Thou record of repentant woe,
All thou askest is contrition
   Thy gifts on mortals to bestow.

CLEMENCY.

Worthy of all praise and glory,
    And worthy of all songs divine;
Worthy monumental story,
    And worthy the immortal line;

Worthy the renown of heaven—
    All praise that angels can bestow,
Sweetest boon to mortals given,
    Oh, consecrate our lives below!

HUMILITY.

DEEP in the earth are treasures found,
　　Costly gems from mines are taken;
The richest notes at eve resound
　　When Philomel's sweet notes awaken.

Thus purest gems of thought we'll find
　　In the meekest minds shall enter;
Humility's a gem refin'd
　　That in humblest souls shall centre.

FELICITY.

TELL me, ye ancient sages,
    And men of mystic lore,
Of pre-imperial annals
    Upon the Ægean shore.

Where dwelt that happy being
    Ye ever sought to find
In all the occupations
    Of your inventive mind?

Say, was she found in battle
    'Mid Persian hosts o'erthrown,
When Greece fought for her freedom
    Upon great Marathon?

Where Valor bade defiance
    To every foe and fear,
And your heroic glory
    Resounded far and near?

Or in your country's honors
    Did she assume the name
And laurels of the victor,
    At the Olympic game?

Or at the shrine of Science
    Did she enchain the mind?
Or was she skilled in labor
    Of Grecian Art refin'd?

Or did Anaximander's,
    Or Zeno's laws unfold
The wealth of all her treasures,
    Unbought by stores of gold?

Dwelt she upon Parnassus
    Amid the famous Nine?
Or did she love old Bacchus,
    Low kneeling at his shrine?

*   *   *   *   *

Tell me, ye Roman legions,
    Ye of triumphant tread,
Whose war-inspiring banners
    O'er every land were spread

From Britain's sea-girt islands
   Where pirates roam'd the sea,
To the blue waves rolling slowly
   On sacred Galilee;

Found ye that mystic Being
   In empires overthrown,
In all the martial glory
   And triumphs ye have known?

'Mid all the wealth and splendor
   From distant lands brought home,
Brought ye the sought-for Goddess
   To your imperial Rome?

Or was it but a fancy—
   A vain delusive dream,
To hope that earthly honors
   Bring all the joys they seem?

And ye who plough the ocean—
   Who visit every land
From Melville's icy island
   T' Australia's golden strand;

FELICITY.

Who brave the raging tempests
  Of wind and wave at war,
And court the countless dangers
  On many a sea afar;

Tell me that land Elysian,
  In all your voyage round
Where gladness reigns forever,
  And sorrow is not found!

Where mortals know no sadness,
  Nor evil passions sway;
Nor hopes e'er prove delusive,
  Nor darkness ends the day;

Nor heroes win their laurels
  At War's red shrine of yore;
Nor victors mark their footsteps
  In prints of human gore.

Where man breathes but affection
  And sympathy for man,
And life is inspiration
  Unfolding in her train

FELICITY.

The happiness we long for,
  The joys we never find,
The hopes that do not lure us
  Like phantoms of the mind.

* * * *

Tell me, ye feathered songsters—
  Ye dwellers of the grove,
In all your sunny regions
  Is there no land of love;

No bright abode where sighings
  Nor sorrows ever come,
Nor tears, nor lamentations
  Shall break upon our home?

Alas! there is no region
  On this side of the tomb
Where mortals know no sorrow,
  Where spirits know no gloom:

But in that land celestial
  Beyond the arching skies,
There man shall find that rapture
  To him that earth denies;

There clouds shall never darken
    The portals of that home;
There night shall cast no shadows
    O'er the celestial dome;

There rest shall greet the weary—
    A sweet and sacred rest—
Like th' infant's peaceful slumbers
    Upon the mother's breast;

There joys shall greet the mourners,
    Whose sorrows shall have end
When Time with his afflictions
    No more their steps attend;

There Happiness shall gladden
    With an exceding joy,
Each child of the Redeemer
In Heaven's bright employ.

LOVE.

How much of grief can that one thing call'd Love,
  How much of care, of sorrow, and of pain
From the dominions of the heart remove;
  Begetting harvests like the golden grain
That yearly multiplies its seeds above
  Preceding numbers, ripened by the rain
And sunshine of the skies! O fruit Divine!
And best since thou art God's and God is thine!

O love unfathomed! Thou, in thy desire,
  Didst take thy flight from Glory down to earth,
And tuned the notes of thy immortal lyre
  To man's redemption by thine own great worth,
Thy virtue ceaseless 'mid a ceaseless fire,
  And suffering sorrow for the Spirit's birth.
O thou celestial and seraphic Love!
Thou soul-transforming power of heaven above!

Hope springs on pinions from thy mortal breast,
  And lifts the spirit from its clods of clay,

And wings it upward from its deep unrest
    To brighter visions of eternal day:
And slumbering faith awakes at thy behest,
    And swifter than the sun's meridian ray
Uplifts the waiting heart to worlds on high,
To thy immortal home beyond the sky.

.

FORTUNE.

FICKLE Fortune! thou dost weave
Thy garlands fair but to deceive
Thy worshippers; thy brightest flower
Oft fades within one fleeting hour.

Thou holdest in thy sumptuous reign
A spell that broken gives but pain—
A charm that ends and leaves no more
Than half the will man had before.

Thou art bedeck'd and fair betimes—
A goddess of luxurious climes,
On whose fair brow bright diadems
Resplendent gleam with brilliant gems.

The fabled wealth of Orient lands
Is less than that at thy commands;
At thy gay feast the gods might dine
And mix their nectar with thy wine.

And thou dost wear Love's sweetest smile
The heart's affections to beguile;
Mirth, Joy, and Gladness seem to meet
To pour their treasures at thy feet.

Gay Pleasure marches in thy train,
Grim Av'rice grasps the gilded gain,
Soft Lux'ry lies on beds of ease
Whilst Adulation comes to please.

But like the storm-cloud's flashing light
That piercest thro' the womb of night,
So sudden gleams the fatal lance
That strikes the luckless crown of Chance:

And as if touch'd by magic wand
The treasures fall from thy fair hand;
Dark clouds bedim thine azure sky,
The flowers around thy pathway die.

And now there shades thy brow a frown
More dark, than bright before thy crown;
And fell desire now lights the eye
That beam'd so late with ecstacy.

Fierce Passion stirs the soul of Hate,
Deep Envy rules inveterate,
Sad Sorrow sits with anxious Care
Whilst creeping comes the foul Despair.

Oh, who would woo thee, fickle dame,
So little worth a lady's name,
Now weaving garlands bright to-day
Which thou'lt to-morrow cast away!

HOPE.

DEEPEST anchor of the soul!
  O Hope thou constant guest of man!
Breathes there on earth from pole to pole,
  From sea to sea's majestic span

A heart untouched, unthrill'd by thee;
  That never felt thy magic breath,
Thy power to free, in some degree,
  The soul itself from dread of death?

That never look'd beyond to-day,
  Nor lived for something to be done;
That had no care to cast away,
  That lived but to exist alone?

It may not be. Such life were death,
  Or even such as brutes respire,
But man who breathes that spirit-breath
  Derived from God, lives to aspire.

HOPE.

And Hope thou art the magic fan
   That flames the embers of the soul;
And inspiration gives to man,
   And leads him victor to the goal.

Of every good and great desire—
   Of every victory to be won,
Thou art the soul's celestial fire—
   The charm of life that leadeth on.

And whether thy bright visions fall
   On hearts, by cares and woes oppress'd,
Of rich or poor, of great or small,
   Thou art the same sweet, smiling guest.

Thy voice with Patience's whispers blent
   Teach how to suffer and endure
Of all our life, each dark event,
   And what of happiness secure.

What tho' thy visions sometimes prove
   Delusive dreams of mortal life!
Did not their bright effulgence move
   The heart to better bear the strife?

Did not the distant treasure lend
   A charm that made the labor light?
Does not some blessing still attend
   Each strong endeavor for the Right?

Beam on, beam on effulgent Hope!
   Like Summer's sun to vine-clad hills,
Adown whose bright, embowered slope
   Arise sweet murmurings of the rills.

Beam on, beam on, O heavenly ray!
   Thro' each deep sorrow of the soul.
And nerve each drooping heart to-day
   To brave the tempest for the goal.

THE FLOWERS.

YE bright, ye blooming Flowers!
    Scattered o'er the verdant hills,
Growing 'neath the woodland bowers,
    Listening to the murmuring rills;

Blooming in the deserts lonely,
    Where so seldom mortals stray,
Where the rays of sunshine only
    Now and then upon you play;

Blooming on the lonely mountain,
    When the rocks your vigils keep,
Where the waters of each fountain
    O'er the craggy ledges leap;

Weeping with your heads inclining
    O'er the graves of friends now gone,
When the stars at night are shining
    And you're seen by them alone;

Growing by the rushy river,
    Where look down the bending skies,

THE FLOWERS.

Gilding dew-drops as they quiver
  On you in the bright sunrise;

Dreading, fearing naught of sorrow;
  Full of love and life to-day,
While your petals on the morrow
  By the winds are borne away;

Ye are earthly gems of beauty
  Humbly placed at Nature's head,
Pointing to the path of duty
  As the path that man should tread.

Ye are emblems God hath given
  Of His mercy and His love;
He hath owned you good from heaven,
  And array'd you e'en above

"Solomon in all his glory."
  We shall then your beauty prize,
Reading from the sacred story
  All the grandeur ye comprise.

We shall love ye, O ye flowers!
  Precious gifts to mortals given;
Blooming 'neath our earthly bowers,
Breathing incense of high heaven.

THE ROSE.

FAR in a deep and silent glade,
    Where woodlands cast a sombre shade,
In softest robes of red array'd,
              Grew a rose.

Unseen by eye in this retreat—
A place untrod by human feet—
It did the self-same tale repeat,
              Blooming rose.

And day by day it grew more fair,
Dispensing all its sweetness there
Upon the solitary air,
              Fragrant rose.

Protected by no human hand,
Uncared for in that unknown land,
But by the breeze of heaven fann'd,
              Bloom'd the rose.

THE ROSE.

Refreshed by sunlight and by dew,
And kissed by favoring winds that blew,
There in its blushing beauty grew
          Summer's rose.

Till day by day, in slow decay,
Its withered leaves all lifeless lay;
And thus this floweret passed away,
          Lovely rose.

O faithless soul! here may'st thou read
A lesson in the lowly mead:
'Tis Heaven supplies thine every need
          And clothes the rose.

He, who hath fashioned it so fair,
Supplied with sunlight, dew, and air,
Would sooner shield our souls from care
          Than deck the rose.

Then let us each with trusting grace,
Tho' low and humble be our place,
Turn heavenward a smiling face
          E'en as the rose.

THE WATER-LILY.

SWEET Lily, fair Lily, bright gem crystalline!
　No blossom is blooming that's purer than thine;

No flower has opened, so pure and so fair,
Such petals of crystal to sun and to air;

Nor ever such sepals of vanishing green
As those on thy border that form thee a screen.

On waters smooth-flowing thy calyx reclines,
While golden beams kiss thy majestical lines;

The ripples that move on the breast of the stream
Disturb thee but like the sweet flow of a dream;

And gently inclining—more stately than grave—
Thou bathest thy breast in each amorous wave.

Far down in the waters, so silent and free,
Thy roots are imbibing sweet potions for thee—

THE WATER-LILY.

Sweet potions that climbing thy sun-seeking stem,
Give beauty and grace to the stream's brightest gem.

Shall flower bloom ever that's fairer than thine,
Thou feature artistic of skill that's divine?

The moonbeams repose on thy virginal breast
As night-waves are lulling thee slowly to rest.

And stars, looking down from the blue, arching skies,
Are smiling on thee with their heavenly eyes.

Bright Morn, from the east, with the wings of a dove,
Comes bearing to thee her fresh greetings of love;

*E'en God has acknowledged thy beauty to be,
But man for a moment looks careless on thee.

* To be taken in a general sense. The lily of Scripture is not the water-lily.—J. E. P.

THE STARS MAY SHINE.

THE stars may shine like rays divine
   On winding rill and river,
The moon's bright beams may gild the streams
   As they roll on forever ;

Aurora, too, may swift renew,
   When night shall end the story
Of love and dreams, her golden beams
   In rose-hued robes of glory ;

The sea at rest with peaceful breast,
   Calm at the hour of even,
May mirror deep in her sweet sleep
   The myriad host of heaven ;

The flowers may greet in language sweet,
   With fragrance and with beauty,
The sparkling dews while earth renews
   To them this nightly duty

But nevermore, as oft before,
  The moon's bright beams discover,
At eventide by the river's side
  The waiting, anxious lover;

For nevermore, as the night-winds soar
  With fragrance richly laden,
At evening hour in the vine-clad bower,
  He meets the dark-eyed maiden.

No more the bliss of love's sweet kiss—
  No more love's sweet caresses!
And no more now love's plighted vow—
  No more love's dear addresses!

The moon shall mourn with him forlorn
  Besides the silent river,
Whose waters lave the lonely grave
  Of her that's gone forever.

WOMAN'S INFLUENCE.

TO MISS M. M.

WHAT bliss that private life attains,
    How happy is that earthly lot,
    How blest to man that sacred spot
Where woman's genial influence reigns!

In whatsoever sphere we move,
    However low in fortune cast,
    This treasure is by none surpass'd—
The treasure of a woman's love.

How desolate and dark that home
    Within whose heaven-forsaken halls
    Fair woman's footstep never falls,
And woman's accents never come!

But bless'd beyond the power to tell
    Is that bright home of mortals here,
    Where woman in her destined sphere
E'er wields her mystic influence well.

WOMAN'S INFLUENCE.

The fairest form that God has made,
    The sweetest grace that he has given
    Beneath his own eternal heaven,
Is that in her fair form array'd.

And hers the power to soothe the heart,
    When cares perplex the wearied mind
    To fortune's ills oft unresign'd
When gloomy doubts their fears impart.

And hers that influence nobler far
    That wields a magic power to move
    The soul to noblest deeds of love,
Surpassing all the deeds of war.

And hers high Heaven's honored trust
    To weave around life's tender years
    That deep affection, that endears
A mother's name to memories just;

That lives thro' each embitter'd strife
    Beyond the limits of our youth,
    A soul-reclaiming, God-like truth
Firm woven in our heart's best life.

And hers the secret power again
  That works by feelings that combine
  To tone, to soften, and refine,
The ruder, sterner moods of men;

That gives to beauty half its grace,
  That gives to virtue half its charm,
  That gives to truth a mighty arm
To elevate the human race.

Not hers the power with warlike hand,
  Where foemen meet on battle-field
  Array'd with armour, sword and shield,
In war to serve or to command.

Not hers the power 'gainst wind and wave
  To plough the fierce relentless sea,
  Or in the conflict's rivalry,
Amid the carnage to be brave.

Not hers Olympus' olive crown,
  Nor any such contested gem;
  But hers a nobler diadem
That yet shall win as fair renown.

Not hers the task where toil demands
   The firmer nerve and sinew strong,
   And harder muscles that belong,
By nature's laws to stronger hands.

But in each higher, nobler race,
   Whether in thought or art refin'd
   That edifies the human kind,
There she with man may find a place.

Behold De Stäel's and Hemans' fame!
   What Browning, Cook, and Stowe have
      wrought,
   What laurels Charlotte Brontë brought
To make immortal woman's name!

The land of letters, love, and lore,
   The land that fought for Helen's wrong
   Immortalized by Homer's song,
That land the name of Sappho bore.

Then deem not man, (if so inclin'd
   A woman's weakness e'er to scorn),

Thyself to nobler duties born
To edify the human kind ;

For hers that noblest gift of heaven,
   That soul-inspiring influence
   Of love, that flows like sweet incense
From some celestial altar given.

IN MEMORIAM,

OF MISS J. M'N——.

YES! death must be some heartless thing,
    E'en thus to so untimely come
    Within the portals of that home,
Where life was blooming in its spring;

Where life, and love, and beauty grew,
    Serene in life's serenest hour,
    Like some rose-tinted spring-tide flower,
Whose modest beauty meets our view.

From childhood's days with joys that teem,
    Her years to youth rolled quickly past,
    With naught of care to overcast
Her future, fair to fancy's dream.

Oh, what a dream is all this life!
    Oh, what an evanescent tide
    Enfolds our lives on every side,
With joys and woes alternate rife!

A few swift-fleeting years at most,
   And night's shade falls upon our shore;
   Our life's sun sets to rise no more,
In death's dark undulations lost:

But long before the narrow sphere
   Of life's allotted days were run—
   Her aspirations but begun,
Death crossed her morning threshold here.

A gift to earth but briefly given—
   The love and joy of kindred dear,
   Nor more shall we behold her here;
She was not born for earth but heaven.

That spirit full of life and love,
   Whose presence cast a brighter spell
   Around the home she loved so well,
Hath gone to brighter realms above.

And here no longer we shall see
   That form symmetric, full of grace;
   That fair and sweetly-featured face,
Once bright with life's serenity.

The smile that lit those azure eyes
    Fond memory now recalls alone;
    The music of that once sweet tone
Shall wake no more its harmonies;

For sickness came to blight life's bloom,
    Spreading o'er cheek, and lip, and eye,
    The death-palor of its dye
To deck an offering to the tomb:

And then at last with peaceful tread
    In that sick chamber, entering slow,
    Death breathed upon her pallid brow,
And left her numbered with the dead.

Alas! to think that she is gone,
    So fair, so young, so beautiful!
    Leaving behind her hearts so full
Of grief, that cannot now atone.

The brightest thought that fills the mind,
    The deepest joy that fills the heart,
    Is oft the swiftest to depart
And leave an aching void behind.

The fairest flower whose lovely bloom
    Doth analyze the living light,
    E'en but to please the sense of sight,
Is oft the first to meet its doom.

But let the heart's grief be resigned
    In this deep sorrow for her loss,
    And patient bear the heavy cross
That Providence hath thus assign'd.

Let resignation to God's will
    The heart's deep sorrow sanctify,
    And point to that bright home on high
Where she hath gone with Christ to dwell.

Death hath but set her spirit free,
    To dwell where death no more shall come,
    Nor sorrow darken her bright home,
Thro' Heaven's blest eternity.

The beams of a celestial light
    To her their radiance now disclose;
    No gloomy clouds shall interpose,
Nor evening draw the veil of night.

No parting farewells shall be said,
    No sound of sorrow there, nor sigh,
    Shall greet that heavenly host on high;
Nor tears of mourning shall be shed.

LOST FEELINGS.

THE day is done; the shadows
   Are now lengthening o'er the lea,
While thro' the leafless branches
   Of the lonely old oak tree,

The wintry winds are blowing
   With a low and mournful dirge,
That greets the lonely hearer
   Like some ocean's midnight surge.

My heart is filled with sadness,
   And this sadness tinged with pain;
These mournful winds have brought me
   To my childhood back again.

And now the thoughts come thronging,
   And a longing grasps my soul;
Oh, would I could unfetter
   These deep yearnings of my soul!

These yearnings for my childhood
   That my spirit cannot calm;
For which no present pleasure,
   And no future finds a balm.

Again I see the valleys
   And the hills in garments green—
Fair Summer's robes of glory,
   And the Autumn's golden sheen.

I see the sunlit waters
   Of fair Simcoe's silver tide,
Fair as some lovely daughter,
   Some new-made happy bride.

I view the crested billows—
   All the white plumes of their waves—
And hear again the music
   That re-echoes from their graves.

I watch the sea-gull flying
   Like a white mist in the wind,
And see the wild duck swimming
   In the beds of rice behind.

LOST FEELINGS.

I join the joyous rambles
   By the forest-fettered lake,
And many a toilsome journey
   Over wild ravine and brake.

I hear the happy voices
   Of the skaters on the shore,
And fancy leaps to join them
   In their revelry once more:

And in each heartfelt measure
   Of these days that seem divine,
There is a music sweeter
   Than the heart can now define.

Oh, radiant days of childhood!
   Brightest sunbeams of my life!
Your sheen has set forever
   On a heart with shadows rife.

Yet not to thee with sorrow
   Yearns my heart, sweet childhood past,
Because that darkened shadows
   With the lights of life were cast.

LOST FEELINGS.

And not to thee, my childhood,
   Shall my thoughts with sadness soar,
Because thy days forever
   Shall return to me no more.

But 'tis because those feelings
   Round the heart no more entwine,
That once made every pleasure
   Of my childhood seem divine.

Ah! yes, the years are fleeting,
   And new joys, new sorrows blend;
New hopes within are rising,
   And new cares our steps attend.

And we may still remember,
   And recount life's pleasure's all;
But Youth's lost feelings never,
We can never now recall.

THE CLOUDS.

BY sunbeams uplifted and lightly wind-drifted
    By the amorous breezes upborne,
And tinged with the hues fair Aurora imbues,
    Float the clouds on the wings of the morn.

They build up their homes in sun-lighted domes
    Both diaphanous, tinted, and clear;
They gild the bright skies when sunbeams arise,
    And at eve when these beams disappear;

They moove smoothly o'er the heaven's' wide floor,
    And so gently go drifting away
All scattered so soon, ere Summer-day's noon,
    By the heat of the bright Summer day;

They gather again their mustering train,
    Nightly round the pale face of the moon;
The stars peep between the rents of their screen
    On the waves of the sky's deep lagoon;

They drink from the rills, the valleys and hills,
    And the river, the lake, and the sea;
They build in the skies their high enterprise,
    And they gladden the earth in their glee.

Wherever they go they have work to do
    For the tree, and the shrub, and the flower;
They weep tempest-toss'd o'er graves of the lost,
    And the rainbow is seen in their shower;

They cast their dark frown o'er country and town,
    And they darken the darkness of night;
The fierce lightnings flash with thundering crash
    From the depths of their caverns of fright;

They bind up their ranks in solid phalanx,
    Cloth'd in shrouds of Tarterean form;
Then open and pour, on ocean and shore,
    The wild fury of tempest and storm.

They cover the scene where Summer grew green
    With a mantle of star-spangled snow;
And piercing and chill, o'er valley and hill,
    Sweep the winds from their caverns that flow.

The sun's levell'd ray in Winter's short day,
  In the depths of their shades they entomb;
And darkly they lower at sunsetting hour,
  Ere the world they enfold in night's gloom;

But sweetly, when earth gives nature new birth,
  And the Spring-notes thro' wild woodlands ring,
Their tears they distil, o'er valley and hill,
  And renew their light robes of the spring.

HOME.

There is a land more dear than all—
   A land fond memories oft recall;
A land for which the heart still yearns
Whatever joys experience earns.
It is that land beneath whose dome
Lies that one sacred spot called home:
There childhood's brief, bright hours were spent;
There life's serenest visions lent
Their brightest charms; there youth's fond dreams
Of life did gild life's silver streams;
There hope like some celestial flower
First blossom'd 'neath that vernal bower.
And there, around that sacred shrine,
Life's first and best affections twine;
There all the dearest ties that life
Can ever form, at once are rife—
Father, mother, daughter, son,
Bound by affections bonds alone.

MAN'S INCONSTANCY.

BEAUTIFUL fields with verdure green;
 Fair forest hills where roll between
The babbling stream, the murmuring rill,
Which with their music once more fill
The mind with thoughts on days of yore
When all was bright life's way before;

Beautiful vales, beautiful glades,
Serenely silent summer shades,
With all the scenes that they recall;
The loves that did our hearts enthral,
The joys that now no longer last,
The hopes that number with the past:

Beautiful flowers, bright and fair,
That waft sweet fragrance on the air,
And paint the fields with richest dye,
As gild the stars the evening sky:
Fair Nature's fragrant, sweet-lipp'd flowers,
Bright gifts of Summer's rose-wing'd hours;

Beautiful heaven of azure blue
That witnesses the Spring renew
Her vernal charms, and Nature give
Her glories here again to live;
Ye are the emblems we may see
Of this world's love and constancy!

Awhile the verdure green shall live;
Awhile the flowers their fragrance give
Awhile the trees their fruits shall bear,
And all her charms fair Nature wear,
But soon their worth life's change shall prove
'Tis thus with friendship, faith, and love.

O inconstant, faithless man!
Read thou thy life in Nature's plan,
And see in all the changes there
The semblance thy affections bear;
Then learn to place thy trust above
In the unchanging God of love!

MEMORIES.

ARISE, ye by-gone memories—
　　Sweet memories of the past,
Return the tuneful melodies
　　That once were round me cast;

Return the heartfelt harmonies
　　Of each enraptured theme,
And all the golden galaxies
　　Round Childhood's life that stream;

The softly-sighing summer breeze
　　That whispered thro' the pine,
And yellow needles from their trees
　　Cast down on beds of vine;

The wild-bird's tuneful minstrelsies
　　That waked the woodland bowers,
The murmuring hum of busy bees
　　Among the summer flowers;

Return the joyful ecstasies
    That filled my childhood's heart,
The sweet, intense felicities
    Of Childhood's guileless art;

Return, ye golden memories,
    Fond Youth's delightful dream,
That filled the soul with melodies,
    Far sweeter than they seem;

Return life's sacred symphonies—
    The cherished friends of yore—
Youth's spirit and its sympathies,
    And I shall ask no more.

Alas! ye by-gone memories,
    Sweet memories of the Past,
Ye are the echoing elegies
    Of joys that could not last.

Ye are the mournful melodies,
    Too deep for human tears,

That tell in measured monodies
    The death of Childhood's years

Ye are the sweet sad mysteries
    That blend the here and there;
That tell in human histories,
    We are not what we were.

SPRING.

CLOTHED with bright robes, O blooming Spring!
What joyful days dost thou rebring!
At thy approach stern Winter flees
To hold his reign 'mid northern seas;
Bright blooming flowers spring to birth
To re-adorn the 'wakening earth;
Unfettered streamlets babbling run
Bright gleaming to the glowing sun.

All thro' the fields of ice and snow
In the wake of Winter fading slow,
Camest thou to spread thy mantles green
Where desolate the fields have been;
Cam'st thou all in thy youthful pride
To bid the unchained waters glide,
To bid from southern climes appear
The feathered songsters of the year.

And thou hast spread a brilliant scene
O'er each fair hill and valley green:—

SPRING.

Clothing the leafless forests bald
With gorgeous crowns of emerald;
Scattering with unsparing hand
The million gems that deck each land;
Breathing the sweetness of thy fragrant breath
On blooms thy voice recalled from death.

Then waft thy fragrance, gentle Spring;
Thy melodies enchanting sing;
Thy glorious visions forth display
To the enraptured gaze of day;
Thy smile that greets the teeming earth
Shall woo new beauty into birth;
While all the earth, and air, and sea,
Shall waft responsive love to thee.

INDIAN SUMMER.

THERE is a time—a pleasant time—
   When Autumn's foremost leaves are falling;
When Autumn's sun shines bright above,
And dreamy shadows softly move
Like spirits round old Summer's grove,
   Old Summer's days serene recalling.

There is a time—a pleasant time—
   When bright the maple trees are glowing;
When soft, cerulean skies look down
Upon the mountain's shades of brown,
Upon the woodland's gaudy crown,
   Upon the river gently flowing.

There is a time—a pleasant time—
   Ere Winter's bleak, cold winds have driven
The pure white snows o'er the frozen ground;
Ere the rippling rills are all ice-bound,
And songs of the feathered race resound
   No more at rosy dawn or even.

'Tis when the hills are all aglow;
   When sunbeams in the valley meeting
Shall kiss the streams they'll know no more,
And the fairest gems that Nature bore
Shall fade and die, as the songsters soar
   To sunnier lands that wait their greeting.

MORN.

THE daylight comes: the shades of night
    Are fleeing fast before the sun,
And with the flood of golden light
    The birds their carols have begun:
High o'er the meadows green and bright
    (Where silvery brooklets silent run),
And o'er the dark pine's tow'ring height
    The rose-hued clouds are floating on.
The air resounds with many a lay;
    And Nature clad in garments green,
And sparkling with full many a gem
Awakes to greet the dawn of day,
    Bright heralded with golden sheen
That floats from Orion's diadem.

GARFIELD—A SONNET.

GREAT Cæsar, noblest in the Roman State—
  The author, soldier, statesman of his time
Did Treason's bloody hand assassinate.
  Again doth History twice repeat the crime;—
First, Lincoln, worthy to be called the Great,
  The martyr to his own life-deeds sublime;
And now again in fair Columbia's land—
  The home of freedom and of equal rights—
James Garfield falls by the assassin's hand:
  Wherever honored Fame shall cast her lights,
By whatsoever breeze of heav'n fann'd,
No brighter beacon o'er the world shall flame,
  Nor find, 'mid records of unceasing flights
Amid mankind, a brighter, nobler name.

INDIA.

HAIL, sultry land of the Hindoo!
    Fair land of British empire too!
Where Himalayan peaks of snow
Look down to burning vales below;
Where far-famed Ganges' waters roll
The fabled way to Heaven's goal;
Where Punjaub's rivers in their pride
Unite to form great Indus' tide.

Hail, land in nature unsurpass'd,
Thou famous store of riches vast!
Wherein the most divergent thrones
Of nature mingle varied zones;
Where fadeless snows of centuries
O'erlook eternal Summer seas;
And vegetation springs to birth,
The guest of unrequited earth.

Hail, too, primeval Hindostan,
Thou fabled home of first-born man!

In thy poetic myths we trace
The genius of thy early race,
The high creative thought attain'd,
The flight of fancy unrestrain'd;
And in thine arts and arms we see
Thine ancient Aryan rivalry.

Hail, land! that on a later day
Thine Indian valor did display,
When thy assembled legions met
The greatest foe that ever yet
The world has known; nor met in vain,
Tho' beaten back with countless slain,
For duty won that day for thee
A nobler name than victory.

Hail, land of still more fair renown,
Thou brilliant gem of England's crown!
Whose high emprise allured in vain
The Eagle's eye with lustful gain;
Whose towers of strength and treasure fill
The ravenous eyes of Europe still;
But yet secure, whate'er is lost,
Beneath the rule thou lovest most.

Soon may thy children trust no more
To pagan gods and Brahmin lore!
Soon may the slavish curse of Caste
Break one by one thy fetters vast,
Till each enfranchised Sudrah find
An equal right with all mankind;
And Superstition's shattered throne
Shall fall beneath the Gospel tone!

BATTLE OF THE PLAINS OF ABRAHAM.

'TIS midnight, and a silence deep
    Now reigns around the fortress keep—
The rocky, rugged, rising steep—
        Of old Quebec.
And in this solemn, silent hour,
And like some vast baronial tower,
It high uplifts defiant power
        'Gainst battle-wreck.

And now, methinks, a time like this,
No watchman guards the precipice
On whose lone tops the breezes kiss
        The *fleur-de-lis;*
For dismal now those rocks arise,
E'er leading upward to the skies,
All seeming proof against surprise
        Of enemy.

And slowly past the fortress steep
Rolls old St. Lawrence dark and deep ;

Whilst all things on its borders sleep,
Save here and there the sentries keep
      Their lonely guard;
And save from out a lonely cove
Wolfe's brave battalions silent move,
And clinging, climb the rocks above
      With whisper'd word.

Far up the heights the band ascends,
Whilst Night their daring deed befriends,
And shaded heaven above them bends
      Her canopy;
And wearied, worn, and broke of rest
The live-long night that rocky breast
They scale, at morn on its high crest
      Perchance to die.

But now Aurora's banners chase
Night's fleeting shades with quick'ning pace,
And ushers in with radiant face
      Effulgent day;
And on The Plains the army stands
In war's array, while Wolfe commands
The men amid whose battle-bands
      Lurks no dismay.

BATTLE OF THE PLAINS OF ABRAHAM.

No soldier there upon the height
May fear the morn's effulgent light,
Or dread the charge, or think of flight,
Who scaled the rocks at dead of night
    The foe to meet :
Each Briton breathes the proud decree
Of ancient Spartan chivalry,
That fears not fate nor destiny—
It is but death or victory,
    But not defeat.

And fast the must'ring foemen form
Like gathering clouds of coming storm :
    With deep dismay
Brave Montcalm views on Quebec's plain—
The rock he deem'd no foe might gain—
The martial host in battle-train
    Of war's array.

In loud alarm the trumpets beat :
The rocks resound with hurrying feet ;
In eager haste the squadrons meet
To hurl defiance and defeat
    Upon the foe.

And now brave Montcalm's valiant breast
Fills with misgivings and unrest—
Prophetic shadows that forcast
    Approaching woe.

But hush ! hark ! the battle-sound
Reëchoes these wild rocks around—
Primeval heights, and depths profound—
    Whence fierce and far,
Now leap's the cannon's lightning flash,
Loud belching forth with thund'ring crash
    The notes of War.

And deeper, deadlier than before,
Far up St. Lawrence rocky shore
Reëchoes the tumultuous roar—
    The loud acclaim
Of battle ; while the lurid lights
Of death, flash, like the fiery flights
Of meteors on Autumn nights,
    Their ceaseless flame.

And lo ! amid the valiant band
With 'kerchief round his blood-red hand,

Brave Wolfe still leads and gives command;
    And meets the foe
With English heart that will not yield
Britannia's sword on sea or field;
Whose daring deeds her fame shall shield
    In weal or woe.

But see! he falls! the life-blood streams
From out his breast! and death's pale beams
Are shadowing now the hero's dreams
    Of victory!
Nay, not the dreams! these battle-cries
Proclaim him victor ere he dies;
Nor death to him the sound denies,
    "They flee! they flee!"

Then back reclined the drooping head
And peacefully the spirit fled;
The voice was hushed, the hero dead,
    His duty done.
And thus came death like sweet repose,
O'er that immortal deed to close
That placed the banner that arose,
And waves still proudly over those
    Grand Heights *he* won.

And from the battle's fierce affray
Where wounded and unhorsed *he* lay,
The brave but vanquish'd of the day,
Who would have held his foe at bay—
The brave Montcalm—is borne away
  Ere long to die;
For ere the morrow's sun shall deck
The rising turrets of Quebec,
Or gild the Plains of battle-wreck,
Upon the soldier's soul shall break
  Eternity.

But in the convent's calm repose
Let there the warrior's labors close:
Let him who fought his country's cause,
Beloved by friends, esteemed by foes,
  Bright laurels deck,
With him who won a victor's grave;
Whose deeds, like Brock's, shall nerve the brave
While on the heights these banners wave,
Placed there by him who dying gave
  To us Quebec.

WATERLOO.

IN the pride of his glory Napoleon rode forth
    With his legions to conquer the foe of the North—
With his veterans to force the red ramparts that lay
Now obstructing to Brussels his war-wending way.

He had swept like an eagle the Alp's rugged ridge,
And had planted his standard on Arcola's bridge;
Like Cambyses of old with his war-waging host,
He had sailed for mad conquest to Egypt's dark coast;

Where the Orient's crash and the cannon's loud roar,
The wild war-cry and death-shriek reëchoed on shore,
Were all blended in battle on Aboukir's wave;
Lurid scene of destruction—dark tomb of the brave.

He had conquered at Austerlitz: Jena did win
His war-thundering march to the courts of Berlin;
And again he had broken the sword and the shield
Of imperial Austria, on Wagram's dread field.

All the nations with wonder and some with dismay
Had beheld his mad march in the Russian assay;
But the grasp of the Spoiler for the old Spanish crown,
Had but brought to old England triumphant renown.

They had seen him in exile at rest from his arms;
They had heard the wild peal of fresh warlike alarms,
When with wings from the limits of lone Elba's isle,
This dread Phœnix arose from War's funeral pile.

Now, again, the brave legions to victory led—
War-veterans of France—to this Spoiler have sped,
Whose battalions now march in war's dread array,
In hot haste to the battle and fierce for the fray.

But the Valor of England is gathering too,
With her war-forces must'ring on famed Waterloo;
And her glory and duty to-day on that field,
Is the fame and the fate of the nations to shield.

Honored Duke of all nations, thou world-famous man!
Oh, let wisdom to-day give thee counsel and plan!
Let thy valor stand firm as the rocks of the sea,
For the fate of Old England is hanging on thee!

Now begins the wild strife, and tumultuous Mars
Now pours forth in fierce battle the climax of wars,
With the flash, and the crash, and the thundering boom
Of the cannon loud-sounding its death-pealing doom.

And the veterans of France pouring forth on her foes
All the might of their strength, all the weight of their woes,
In the grandest of efforts this mightiest day
Since the legions of Cæsar o'er Pompey held sway.

And the heat of the contest increasing each hour,
As the tide of the tempest with wild-surging power
Is repelled from the lines in each furious dash,
And the steed and his rider reel back with a crash.

But again, and again, and again to the course
Rush the troops of the Despot with redoubled force,
In a struggle that lasts thro' the heat of the day,
'Mid the clash, and the roar, and the smoke of the fray.

Oh! behold the wild wreck of each terrible shock!
And the valor of England, that, firm as the rock

Of her own native isle, meets the force of each blow
With her Saxon defiance hurled back on the foe.

With her stubborness stemming the war-waves of France,
Wildly dashing their sea-foam of sabre and lance—
Wildly pouring their torrents like tempests of hell
On the ranks growing thinner with fierce shot and shell.

Thus the Gaul and the Briton, with cannon and steel
In a death-tug for victory, now loudly appeal
With the voice of their arms to the god of their might—
The one loud for Ambition, the other for Right.

In the heat of the struggle and wail of its woe,
In the clash and the crash of the arms of each foe,
Which shall win? Shall Ambition hurl down
On this field the Defender of England's renown?

Not one foot to the foe on this day shall he yield!
Not one leaf of his laurels shall fall on this field!
But all nations shall ring with the deeds of the day,
That his valor eclipsed both Napoleon and Ney.

Now ring out, ye deep thunders, upon the wild air
The fierce war-notes of Blucher, that peal from afar!
For your sound is the summons of heaven's decree
That on Waterloo's field shall the nations be free!

And the sound of that cannon like a requiem rolls
O'er the soul of Napoleon its death-pealing tolls;
And with efforts gigantic again to the fray,
Like a tide of the ocean, sweeps war-renowned Ney.

But again with disaster, and desperately foil'd,
Has the Guard of French glory all broken, recoil'd
From the ranks that have dash'd, like the rocks of
    the sea
Into deep-seething foam the wild waves in their glee.

Hark! with cheers now ascending the wild-welkins ring,
And as swift as an eagle with air-cleaving wing,
On the war-baffled foe, like a bolt from the sky,
Sweep the bayonets of England to conquer or die.

They have pierced like an arrow the heart of that host,
And the last hope of victory for France has been lost;
Battle-broken, and conquer'd, and rapidly cast
From that field, like the leaves in the Autumn's wild
    blast.

ALEXANDRIA.

IN the harbor east and west
    Lay the ironclads at rest—
Britain's bulwarks of the sea—
With their cannon landward prest,
With their streamers floating free,
With their seamen to contest
    Once another foe by sea.

There was silence dead as night
Brooding o'er the solemn sight
    As the day-beams lit the sky;
As the hours in their flight
Brought from Egypt no reply,
Till the summons for the fight
    From the signal-ship did fly:

Then from bursting shot and shell
Such tumultuous thunders fell,
    Crashing with such loud reports,

That it seemed both heaven and hell
Had combin'd to storm the forts:
Had combin'd to crush and quell
   All the lines along the ports.

British tars as brave and bold,
As were those who fought of old
   Under Nelson at the Nile,
On that day new fame unroll'd
For Britannia's sea-girt isle;
And in tones of terror told
   Deeds of wonder all the while.

All that day against the walls
Thunder'd forth resistless balls
   From the heavy armor'd fleet:
Heard in Cairo's frighted halls;
Heard in Malta's far retreat;
Heard where fierce the missile falls
   On the war-doom'd city's street.

Loudly did the war begin;
Ceaseless roll'd its deadly din
   O'er the land and o'er the sea;

O'er the ruin'd Ras-el-Tin
Where the Crescent floated free;
Till the Cross that day did win
   Its triumphant victory.

Where the deadly shot and shell
Round each fort and fortress fell
   There was ruin to behold:
There was death in every knell
From the British cannon toll'd,
Till a terror, as of hell,
   Seiz'd the bravest and most bold;

Till no more the fort guns peal'd,
And the city's fate was seal'd;
   Till the shattered ramparts flew
Flags of truce, and backward reel'd
From the forts the rebel crew,
And beneath the traitor's shield
   From the city's gates withdrew.

Not a ship of all the line
Sank that day beneath the brine;
   Not a gun had England lost

At the famous day's decline :
And of all her naval host—
Out of all her gallant line
   Five brave lives the conflict cost.

Such was Seymour's brave command ;
Such was was England's gallant stand
   There before the rebel crew :
Every action nobly plann'd,
Nobly plann'd and carried thro'
By that brave heroic band—
   England's gallant naval crew.

CHARGE OF THE HIGHLAND BRIGADE AT TEL-EL-KEBIR.

INTO the trenches, sword and sabre,—
    Into the trenches with a crash,
There on the Plains of Tel-el-Kebir,
    Hotly the Highland soldiers dash.
Bullets around them roll and rattle;
    Bayonets around them gleam and flash;
There in the heat and tide of battle—
    There as they sabre, cut, and clash.

They are the first to win new glory,
    Meeting the Arabs hand to hand;
There in the trenches, red and gory,
    Flashing the claymore's lightning brand;
Doing such feats and deeds of danger;
    Fighting like devils might and main;
There in the face of foe and stranger,
    Heaping the trenches with the slain:

CHARGE OF THE HIGHLAND BRIGADE.

Proving by deeds of warlike wonder
    Britain's brave sons will heroes be;
Silencing Egypt's tones of thunder
    At Tel-el-Kebir, as by sea;
Breaking a nation's chains asunder;
    Setting the slaves of tyrants free;
Crushing the hopes of despots under
    Iron-hoof'd heels of Destiny.

Out of the trenches, sword and sabre,—
    Out of the trenches with a dash;
Into the works of Tel-el-Kebir—
    Into the strongholds with a clash;
Cannon around them roar and rattle;
    Cannon around them boom and crash;
As in the front and tide of battle
    Fiercely the Highland bayonets flash.

Hotly and bravely, Britain's heroes,
    Nobly enacting deeds of fame;
There in the land of war-famed Pharaohs
    Boldly upholding England's name;
Thundering, rushing, dashing, crashing
    Into the cannon's blazing breath;

Into the midst of hell-fires flashing ;
　　Into the jaws and teeth of Death :

Till from the bayonet-point and sabre,
　　Soldiers around then dying lie ;
Till from the works of Tel-el-Kebir,
　　Arabi's legions swiftly fly.
Such was the brief but brilliant story—
　　Such was Sir Garnet's brave command—
Winning new fame for England's glory
　　There on Egyptian plains of sand.

LORENZO.

[This poem was suggested on reading the "Rime of the Ancient Mariner," but those who have read that poem need expect no emulation of that masterpiece of Coleridge. The poem when completed will consist of four parts. For the present only the first part is published.]

PART I.

THE SHIPWRECK.

A SHIP at sunrise leaves the shore
    For a port in a foreign land:
Each man to landward looks once more,
    And grasps each kinsman by the hand.

Each farewell said, the sails are set,
    And fast the ship sails in the wind;
While on the shore are weeping yet
    The hearts of those they've left behind.

But one alone—a maiden fair—
    More sad than all the rest doth seem;
And still she stands and gazes there
    As one who looks when in a dream.

Is it a sister or a brother
    That keeps her on the shore so long?
Or, dearer still, is it a mother
    On whom her thoughts are fixed so strong?

The ship sails on past islands green—
    Bright emeralds rising from the sea—
But never stays for aught that's seen:
    Like a white gull in the wind sails she.

She swiftly skims the ocean-tide,
    And soon has lost her native shore;
And many a league the waters wide
    Divide her from the land before.

All day with never a change of speed,
    With whitle sails gleaming in the sun,
Like the race of an Arabian steed,
    The vessel swift its course did run.

Then sank the golden sun to rest
    Beneath the western waves afar;
And from the ocean's boundless breast
    Uprose the moon and twilight star.

And all above was the shining train
    That fleck'd the deeps of heaven's dome;
And all around was the surging main,
    And dashing spray of white sea foam.

A youth on deck walk'd to and fro—
    Walk'd with a slow and measur'd pace;
A youth of sixteen years and two,
    With a handsome girlish-featur'd face;

A maidenly figure, medium height,
    Complexion that of a southern clime;
Dark eyes that flash'd a lustrous light,
    And locks that graced Hyperion's prime.

Lorenzo slowly paced the deck,
    And fix'd upon the waves his eyes;
And sadly watch'd the moon-beams break,
    And sadly saw the full-moon rise.

What joy can glancing eyes behold
    When sorrow keeps the heart confin'd?
What pleasure can the world unfold
    When that we love is left behind?

And he had left his native home,
    The fond retreats of happy hours;
And her with whom he loved to roam
    Beneath Cordova's verdant bowers:

In blooming vales of orange grove
    When evening cool'd the sun-god's fever,
They'd met and told their plights of love,
    Or as they sail'd the Guadalquiver:

She, a fair maiden, seventeen,
    With dark brown hair and love-bright eyes,
The same who long at the shore was seen
    When sail'd the ship from Port Cadiz.

And were their meetings past forever
    'Mid Andalusia's vales and bowers,
And where the winding Guadalquiver
    Rolls thro' fields of blooming flowers?

The past is like some story told;
    The present lives and breathes revealing;
The future fast its secrets hold,
    Alike the good and ill concealing.

LORENZO.

Sweet sounds ring in Lorenzo's ears,
    Above the waves wild dash and roar;
'Tis the melodious voice he hears
    Of Nora from the far-off shore;

Whose tones came mournful, soft and low,
    As breathes the sweet Æolian string,
When soft winds woo the chords with woe
    On Harmony's enraptured wing.

He saw the fond eyes fill with tears,
    And knew the words she wish'd to tell;
And all for him her doubts and fears,
    And rising sighs she could not quell.

Again in thought he dried her eyes,
    And fondly clasp'd her heaving breast;
And gently sooth'd his Nora's sighs,
    And kissed her anxious fears to rest.

Then breathed a loving and fond adieu,
    And bade her pray that wind and tide
Might bear him swiftly to Peru,
    And back to make her a Spanish bride.

Three days the ship ran in the wind:
    And then a change; and three times three
The veering wind did prove unkind,
    And drove her northward thro' the sea.

Then ceas'd to rage the wind's wild will;
    The waves of the sea all sank to rest;
The white ship lay on its bosom still
    As a child on its mother's breast.

The sails all dropp'd, the pennons fell,
    And never a sound came to the ship;
An ominous silence cast its spell,
    And whispers low came from each lip.

And all around was the glassy sea;
    The sun did glow with heat on high:
No ripple disturb'd the crystal lea;
    No cloud pass'd o'er the burning sky.

And wondrous snakes of green and gold,
    By thousands round the ship were seen
Entwined in many a Gordian fold,
    With hissing tongues, and eyes of green.

And weird, strange shapes did crawl and creep—
   Foul births of burning sun and sea—
Till all the slimy, slumbering deep,
   In one mix'd mass moved loathsomely.

And each day hotter grew the sun,
   And grew each day endurance less;
And each rejoiced when day was done,
   And night relieved the heat's distress.

And every morn Aurora flung
   Her red sheets o'er the eastern wave,
Till hope from every heart was rung;
   The sea must be their silent grave.

For fifteen days the ship did lay,
   Nor moved the sails a single thread,
While raging fever seiz'd its prey,
   And fully five score men lay dead.

They dropp'd the dead men, one by one,
   Like leaden weights into the wave;
And quick the burial task was done,
   As sank each corpse into its grave.

Then came a change: no sun was seen,
    And storm-clouds darken'd all the sky;
The ocean turn'd to deep sea-green,
    The winds arose, the waves roll'd high.

The ship again sprang to its course,
    And swiftly skimm'd the tossing main,
Like the bounding speed of a frighten'd horse,
    Or wild gazelle on Afric's plain;

Or as the hound with keen intent,
    Long seeking the lost trail with care,
When once he finds the well-known scent,
    With doubled speed pursues the hare.

All day upon the waters wide,
    With storm-clouds drifting round the sun,
The ship shot thro' the foaming tide,
    Nor slacken'd once the speed begun.

And oft she reel'd before the blast,
    And seem'd to sink beneath the foam;
Then upward sprang with sail and mast,
    Like a thing that oft defies its doom.

And fiercer blew the raging winds,
 And hollow sounds came from the sea;
And fear came to the mariners' minds
 When the main-mast broke in pieces three.

They scann'd the sea for a single sail;
 But search'd in vain the waters wide;
And night now follow'd the ship's fleet trail,
 And darkness pillow'd the plunging tide.

Around the ship the lightnings play'd;
 As loud the heavenly thunders peal'd
-As if ten thousand warriors made
 The ocean's breast their battle-field;

As if from sleep Hell's legions woke,
 And to the sea-green halls had come,
So great a fury dash'd and broke
 And lash'd the wild waves into foam;

As if the Prince of devils dash'd
 His fierce battalions thro' the air,
So loud the clouds in thunder clash'd,
 So vivid shot the lightnings there:

And still the mariners rode the sea
    Till each in terror held his breath,
Wond'ring what thing the ship could be
    Defying both the sea and death.

Without a sail, without a mast,
    With nothing but the hull alone,
Like some mad devil hurrying fast
    The ship still thro' the waves rode on.

Ten men on deck loud curses spoke,
    And five in prayer did bend the knee;
A high wave o'er the vessel broke,
    And swept the ten into the sea:

Then quickly rose the other five;
    And in their looks were woe and fear,
For each of those that did survive
    Had lost some friend or kindred dear:

And one had lost an only brother—
    The one companion from his birth—
And they from childhood loved each other
    With love that told love's highest worth;

And one had been a wayward child,
    And passionate beyond control;
While the other's words and ways were mild,
    That quickly won the heart and soul;

And him, the fiercer bolder brother,
    The waves had wash'd into the sea,
Whilst deepest sorrow seiz'd the other,
    Who trembling rose from bended knee:

Then down the hold the five did creep,
    Each terror-struck with what had come;
And there five other seamen sleep,
    Unconscious of the approaching doom.

"Awake! awake!" Lorenzo cried,
    "The ship will sink before the morn;
Our comrades sleep beneath the tide,
    And we to them shall soon be borne."

Then one arose with vacant stare
    And watch'd the dim lamp's dying gleam,
And muttering curs'd Lorenzo's care,
    And dozed again into a dream;

And one but raised his heavy head,
    And half unconscious cross'd his breast;
Then slept again like one that's dead,
    So much does death resemble rest;

But never a sound came from his lip,
    Nor sign of life the rest had given
When lightning struck the reeling ship,
    And flash'd o'er all the vaults of heaven.

That moment, toss'd by wind and tide,
    As burst volcanoes wild and free
Thundering missiles high and wide,
    So burst the ship on that wild sea:

And thro' the fierce tormented air.
    'Mid wind and wave's wild revelry
Were hurl'd the wrecks of that once fair
    And stately ship that sail'd the sea.

And loud the pealing thunders crash'd,
    Till shook the dismal domes of heaven;
And high the rolling billows dash'd,
    By all the tempest's fury driven.

Not such a sea, nor such a night
    Had e'er the boldest seaman seen;
Nor ship held ever so long upright,
    Such howling winds and waves between:

Nor e'er was seen so wild a wreck
    On sea or earth, in air or sky,
As on the ocean's breast did break
    That night before the mariner's eye:

And sinking down into the deep—
    Into the deep sea's slimy bed,
The drowsy mariners wake from sleep;
    But wake to mingle with the dead.

Five men are saved, and only five,
    Nor hopes nor hearts for much have they;
For tho' they may the storm survive
    They yet must be grim hunger's prey:

And death rolls near them side by side,
    And leaps, and laughs, and mocks their fears,
Wild dancing round them on the tide;
    And in the lightning's glance appears:

Yet life is sweet; and while we live
    A hope still breathes in every soul—
A hope that stronger nerve can give
    Than will itself can half control:

And so they, struggling, caught and clung
    To planks, or timbers, or whate'er
The fortunes, fates, or demons flung,
    Or dashing waves or winds brought near;

Till o'er the sea the morning dawn'd
    As bright morns dawn in dismal caves;
For thro' the leaden domes beyond
    No sun came to the tossing waves:

But by degrees the high winds fell;
    The billows ceas'd to dash their spray;
Yet still there roll'd a heavy swell,
    And gloomier grew the dismal day;

And heavier hung the heavy clouds,
    Till all the air was but a sheet
Of mist, and fog, and drifting shrouds
    That seem'd congealing into sleet.

Then down the rain in torrents fell,
    Like rivers rolling from on high;
And six long hours, fast and well,
    It drain'd the cisterns of the sky.

The winds were still; the rain had ceas'd;
    The sea's deep surge was settling fast
With gentle sighs, like those releas'd
    When woman's fiercest passion's past.

As woman weeps her anger o'er,
    So wept the ocean reconcil'd;
And round her breast a mantle bore
    Of mist and vapor densely pil'd.

All day the wreckers, weak and wet—
    Half-dead with hunger, drench'd with rain,
At evening felt their last hopes set,
    As sank the sun below the main:

And in the mists and fogs that rose,
    And roll'd their reeking vapors free;
And farther when the night did close,
    They lost each other on the sea:

And each knew not the other's fate;
    And little reck'd they what might be
The last of all the woes to wait
    Upon them on th' unconscious sea.

And dark and dismal was the night;
    The waters echoed a wail of woe;
The sea and death had ceas'd to fright;
    Each mariner's life was ebbing low.

Long ere the eastern grey-streaks cast
    The first faint tokens of the dawn,
Four more from life to death had pass'd,
    And one alone lived faint and wan.

And now the night, retiring, fled,
    And morning met a glowing sky;
The sun rose from the waves, and spread
    Effulgent beams of golden dye.

And with the bright effulgence came
    The sea with gleaming sheets of gold;
While high above her sapphire flame
    Were bright cerulean hues unroll'd.

No fairer sight in all the earth
   Might one behold than that fair sea,
With light waves springing into birth
   As waves the wild-grass o'er the lea.

And hope came to Lorenzo's soul—
   For he from death had rescued been—
That he might reach some island goal,
   Or by some passing ship be seen.

He looks and scans far on the sea
   A something on the ocean's breast,
That with the waves moves listlessly,
   Slow passing the horizon's crest.

A beam, perchance, or broken spar
   On which some comrade still is living,
Drifting slow on the sea afar,
   The waves to it their motion giving.

Perchance some yacht, or small life-boat
   That 'mid the storm some ship set free,
But no! no boat or ship afloat
   Had ever stemm'd that stormy sea.

The object moved upon the tide,
   And glistened in the sun's bright sheen;
Till o'er the dim horizon wide,
   Like fading mist it passed unseen;

Nor in the sky, nor sea across
   Did other object meet the eye,
Except some wandering albatross,
   Or stormy petrel passing by.

Lorenzo dropp'd his heavy head,
   Hard-pillow'd on a sea-rock'd beam;
His eyelids closed like lids of lead;
   He fell asleep into a dream:

And all again was once more bright;
   Glad visions swift pass'd thro' his mind—
Fond visions of his youth's delight
   In lands Elysian left behind:

Again he climb'd the hills of Spain,
   And roam'd her valleys fresh and green;
And once more play'd a boy again
   Where wild flowers deck'd the sylvan scene.

The Bœtis, famed in Roman lore,
    Again did greet his eager eyes,
Beholding, on its shining shore,
    Cordova's domes and spires arise.

And bright lights gleam her streets along;
    Sweet strains of music greet his ear;
He joins the terpsichorean throng,
    With youth's fond friends and loved ones near.

Bright Pleasure beams with kindling eyes;'
    And love transported to his dreams,
Bears on swift wings with sweet surprise
    Fair Nora to his thoughts and themes.

There do, betimes, such trials fall
    As crush the spirit's strongest trust;
That make mere cowards of us all,
    And crumble earth's frail hopes to dust.

And such a trial, e'en as this,
    Lorenzo felt, when from his sleep
Of transient dreams of love and bliss,
    His eye still wandered o'er the deep.

He saw far in the west the sun
   Now sinking in the purple sky;
But heedless of the race it run,
   He closed once more his eyes to die.

Like some weird phantom undefin'd,
   Some strange delusion of the soul,
An image flash'd across his mind,
   And bound him 'neath its strange control.

And e'en until the sun did set
   Strange visions rose before his eyes;
Sometimes the visions of regret,
   Sometimes wild phantoms of surprise:

Now huge fierce monsters of the sea,
   With burning eyes like balls of fire,
Surround him, gamboling in their glee,
   Revealing fangs of keen desire.

Now black sea-serpents round the beam
   Their lengthy bodies tightly lace;
And close and fierce their green eyes gleam;
   Their forked tongues hiss into his face:

And strange forms flit through all the air,
    And skim the waters to and fro;
And wild shrill utterings of despair,
    And demon shrieks come from below:

And thro' the rosy sun-set sky,
    High o'er the sun-kiss'd golden sea,
A skeleton ship flew swiftly by—
    A skeleton ship with sea-maids three;

And one in gossamer robes of white,
    With golden tresses streaming down,
Held o'er the prow a flaming light
    That flashed above her golden crown;

And one like some swarth southern slave,
    With ebon locks and sun-burn'd face,
Did guide the ship on th' ether wave
    In its ærial wind-like race;

And one was a maiden wondrous fair;
    But ne'er such eyes so sad, sublime—
With which but angels might compare—
    Did ever gaze on the woes of time.

The burning sun 'mid the waves went down;
   The spectres all in the twilight fled;
The phantom ship and maids had flown;
   Lorenzo alone lay asleep or dead.

*   *   *   *   *   *

The night is calm, the moon shines bright
   Afar on the deep and slumbering sea;
An isle beneath the veil of night
   Lies sleeping on the crystal lea:

And on the beach, cast on the sand,
   Is something in the moonlight seen;
What can it be on that lone strand,
   The woodland and the sea between?

A lonely maid approaches near,
   And sad the sight she now descries—
There in the midnight cold and clear,
   A colder corpse before her lies.

The maiden gazed on the marble brow,
   And touched the cheeks with finger-tips;
And, won by that fair form, somehow
   A low, faint sigh escaped her lips;

Then bending o'er the lifeless clay,
   Her rose-lips in a trembling quiver,
She kiss'd the cold face as it lay;
   But strange the thrill that kiss did give her:

The pale lips move; a low, faint breath
   Soft as an infant's thro' them flows;
The kiss calls back the soul from death;
   The fingers twitch; the eyes unclose:

The maiden starts with sudden fear,
   And backward steps with piercing scream.
She stops! she looks! again draws near!
   Lorenzo wakes as from a dream.

END OF PART I.

www.ingramcontent.com/pod-product-compliance
Lightning Source LLC
Chambersburg PA
CBHW020133170426
43199CB00010B/734